3D COLORING
Cities

Includes lightly guided doodle pages

Hannah Davies

THUNDER BAY
P · R · E · S · S
San Diego, California

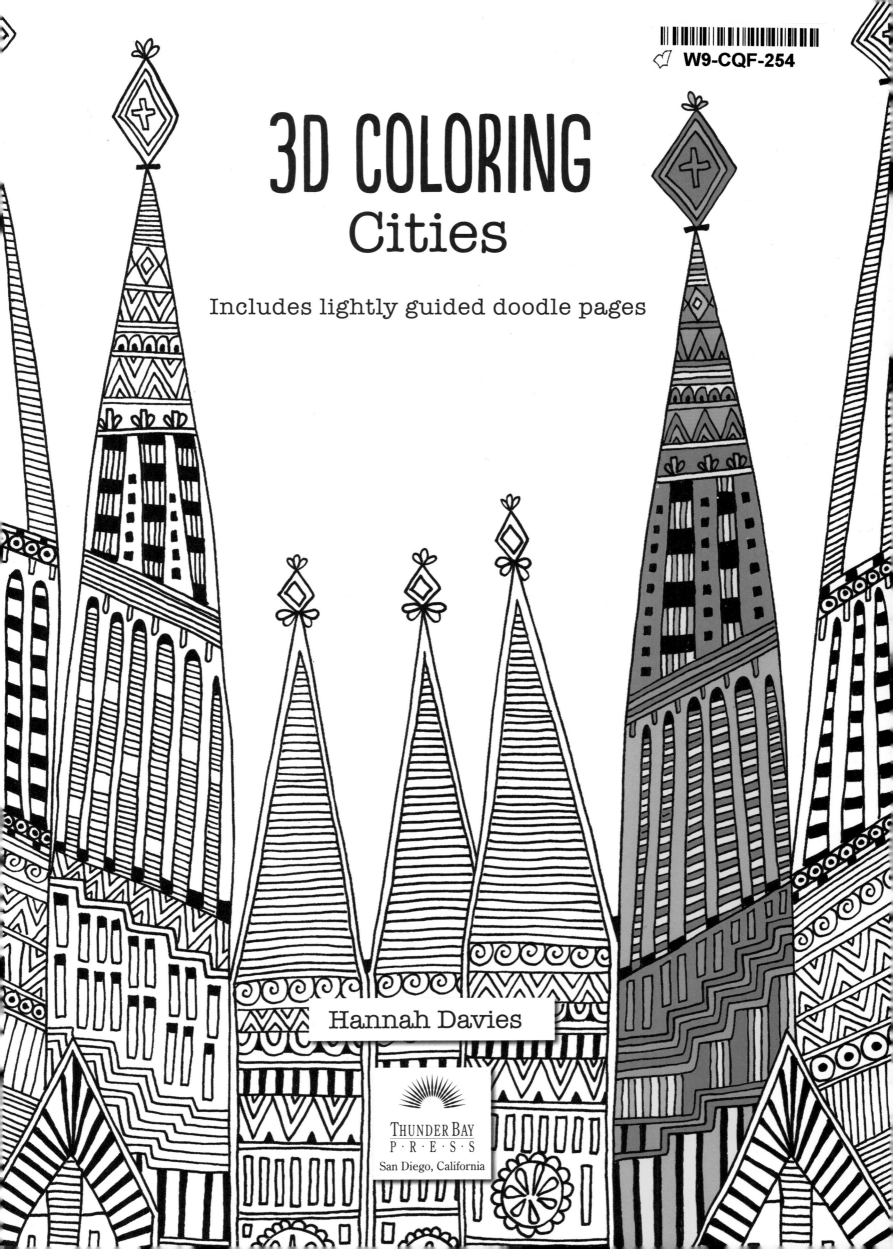

Thunder Bay Press
An imprint of Printers Row Publishing Group
10350 Barnes Canyon Road, Suite 100,
San Diego, CA 92121
www.thunderbaybooks.com

This book was conceived, designed, and produced by
Quintet Publishing Limited
114–116 Western Road
Hove, East Sussex
BN3 1DD
United Kingdom

QTT.3DCI

Quintet Publishing Team:
Project Editor: Alice Sambrook
Designers: Gareth Butterworth, Paula Lewis
Illustrator: Hannah Davies
Art Director: Michael Charles
Editorial Director: Alana Smythe
Publisher: Mark Searle

Thunder Bay Press Team:
Publisher: Peter Norton
Publishing Team: Lori Asbury, Ana Parker, Laura Vignale
Editorial Team: JoAnn Padgett, Melinda Allman

ISBN: 978-1-62686-457-3

Printed and bound in China by RR Donnelley

19 18 17 16 15 1 2 3 4 5

The glasses included with this book are intended only for viewing ChromaDepth® 3D images. Not for extended wear, performing physical activity, driving, or operating machinery. Do not look into the sun with glasses. Manufactured by American Paper Optics, LLC, Bartlett, Tennessee, USA.

This book belongs to

....

CONTENTS

INTRODUCTION

I grew up beside the sea in south Wales. It's a beautiful part of the world with areas of outstanding natural beauty. Spending all these years here has made me the person I am today: creative, colorful, and absolutely obsessed with drawing.

The beaches are untouched, and there are miles of landscape to explore. I walk these beaches twice a day with my old English sheep dog, Charlie, and see so many changes in water patterns, waves, tides, sunsets and sunrises, and also spectacular full moons. The inspirational happenings in nature encourage me to draw day and night, and I can't imagine a day without doodling. If ever you need artistic incentive, I would advise getting outside and absorbing the world around you.

I am fascinated with microscopic patterns and detail, and love creating endless layers and textures, which you will see reflected in the pages of this book. It is a collection of reconceived iconic landmarks, urban metropolises, and sprawling cityscapes from my imagination! The graph paper in-between each design has a little pattern or outline to start you off creating designs of your own.

You can then use your 3D glasses to see the patterns and scenes pop off the page as you color them in. I would suggest applying vibrant watercolor pencils to get the best effect, but felt tip pens are fine too. I hope that this book gives you as much enjoyment experimenting as I have had creating it. Happy coloring in 3D!

If you love this book, why not try out the others in the series, *3D Coloring Flowers* and *3D Coloring Animals?*

HOW TO COLOR IN 3D

Included in this book, you will find a pair of ChromaDepth® 3D glasses that use the latest in stereoscopic technology to create an amazing illusion of depth in hand-drawn images.

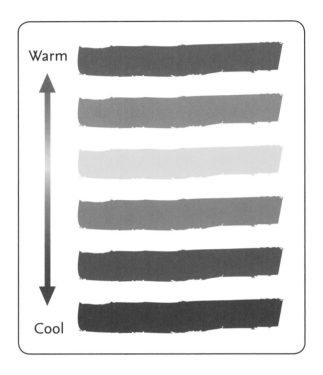

- Use cool colors for parts that you want to banish to the background. Use warm colors for parts of a drawing that you want to come forward and appear as if they are floating up off the page.

- Follow the color-chart at the left if you need a quick reminder of what cool and warm colors are.

- Whether you pick out small details and bring these to the foreground or choose to feature larger areas does not matter. It's all about experimenting to see what looks groovy.

- This book also includes graph paper, so get inspired and create your own illustrations.

Note

We recommend that you use bright watercolor pencils or felt tip pens to achieve the best possible effect.

Tips

Tint
Bold, bright colors appear the most 3D. The lighter the colors, the more they will lie toward the middle of the spectrum and will neither jump forward nor move back much at all. However, you can use lighter tints effectively alongside bold colors to add texture to dark backgrounds.

Depth perception and shading
It is possible to enhance the 3D effect created by the glasses through using standard artistic tricks for producing 2D effects. Try shading for roundness, overlapping, adding shadows, increasing the brightness of color on objects closer to the foreground, and changing size as depth changes.

Use of black
Black tends to complement cool and warm colors alike. 3D images would not appear so without the use of black outlines; without them, the colors inhabit an undefined area. Black outlines provide edges for your mind to locate in space, enlarging the apparent depth. Use thicker black outlines for the areas you want to really pop.

Use of white
Whereas black is happy to sit at the front or back of a 3D image, white will always appear in the middleground. This can be useful to provide a central horizon for the warm and cool colors to stand on either side of. Be careful when touching warm colors to the white border though; it may drag them back from the foreground.

DOODLE PAGES

Express yourself with these lightly guided doodle pages.
The suggestive framework will get you started, and the
grid will help you scale and place your drawing. Use the
printed doodles as inspiration and let your creativity flow.
Apply color following the guide on pages 6 and 7 to see
your artwork come to life.

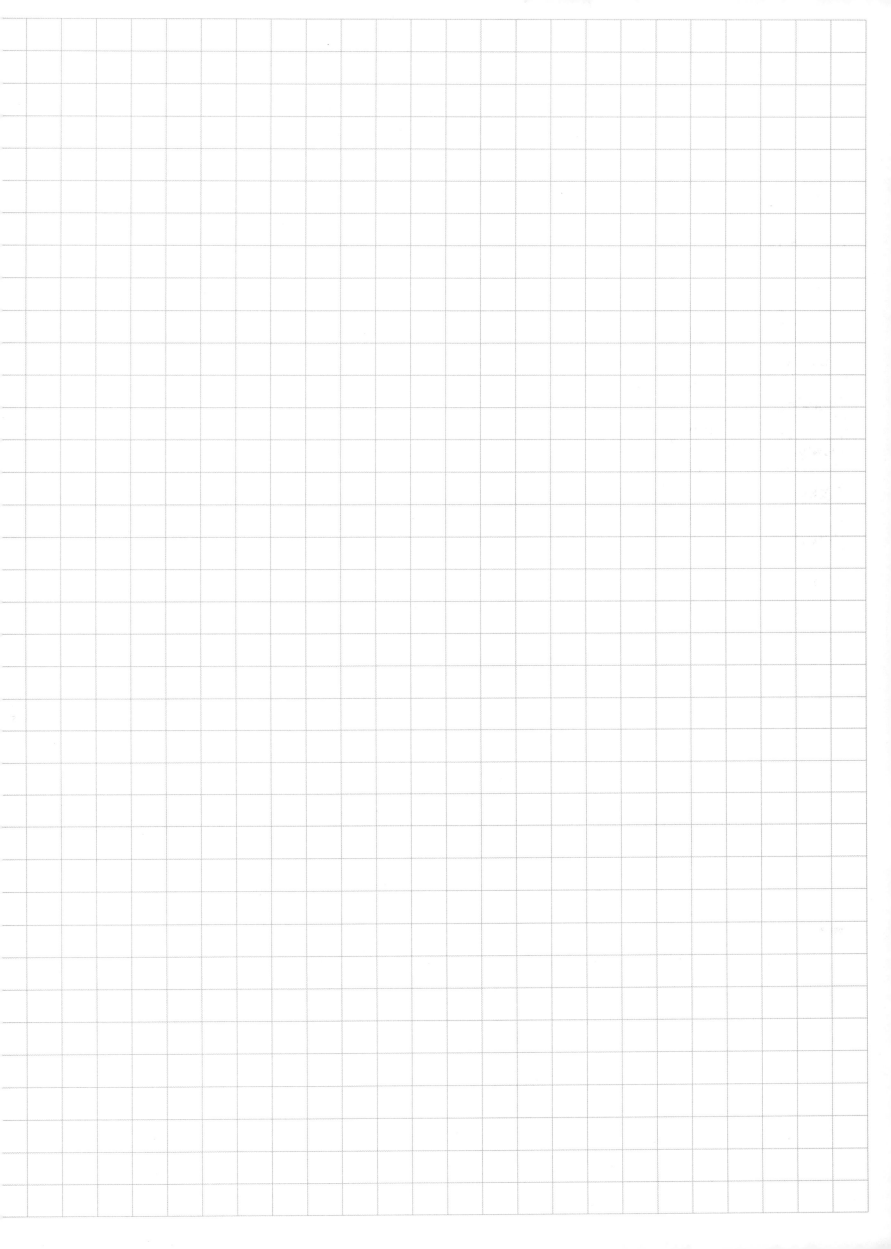

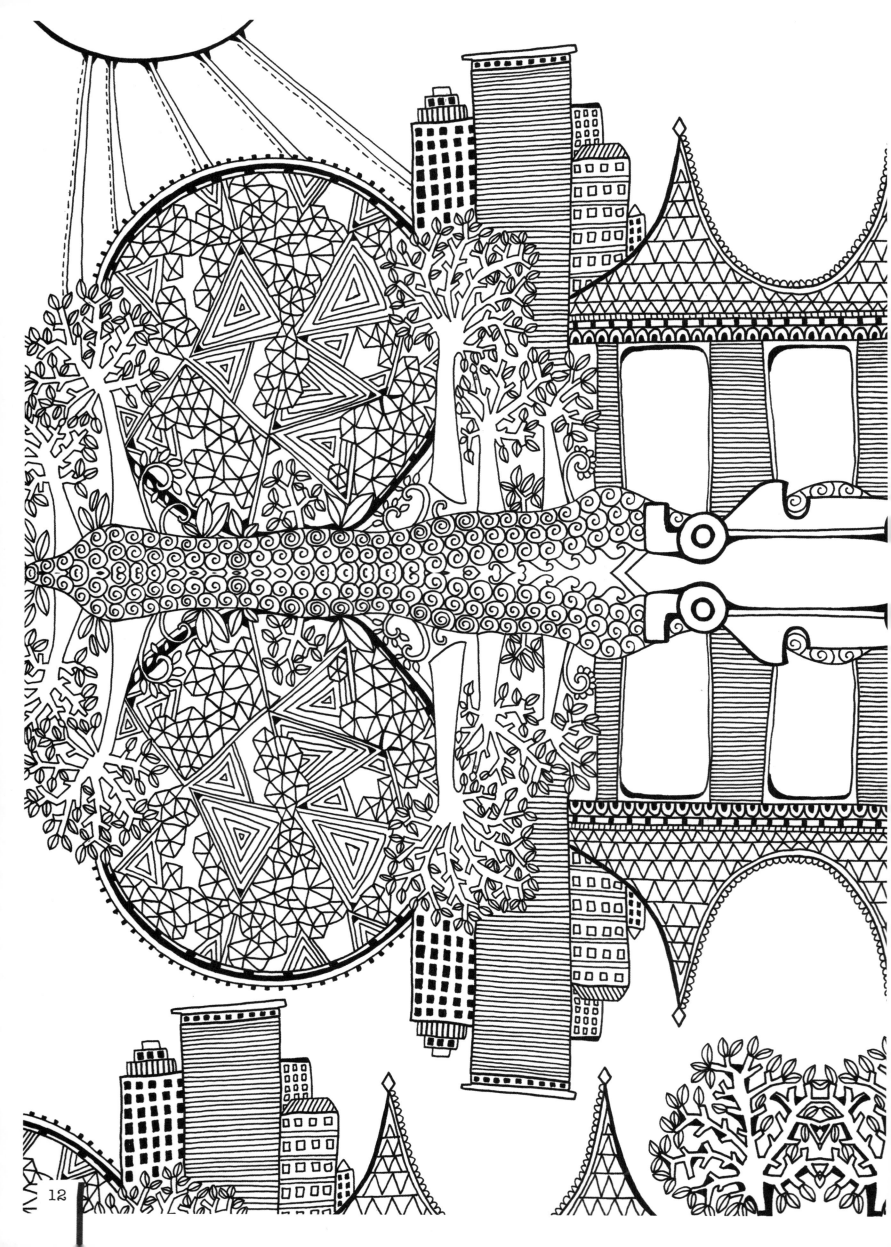

13

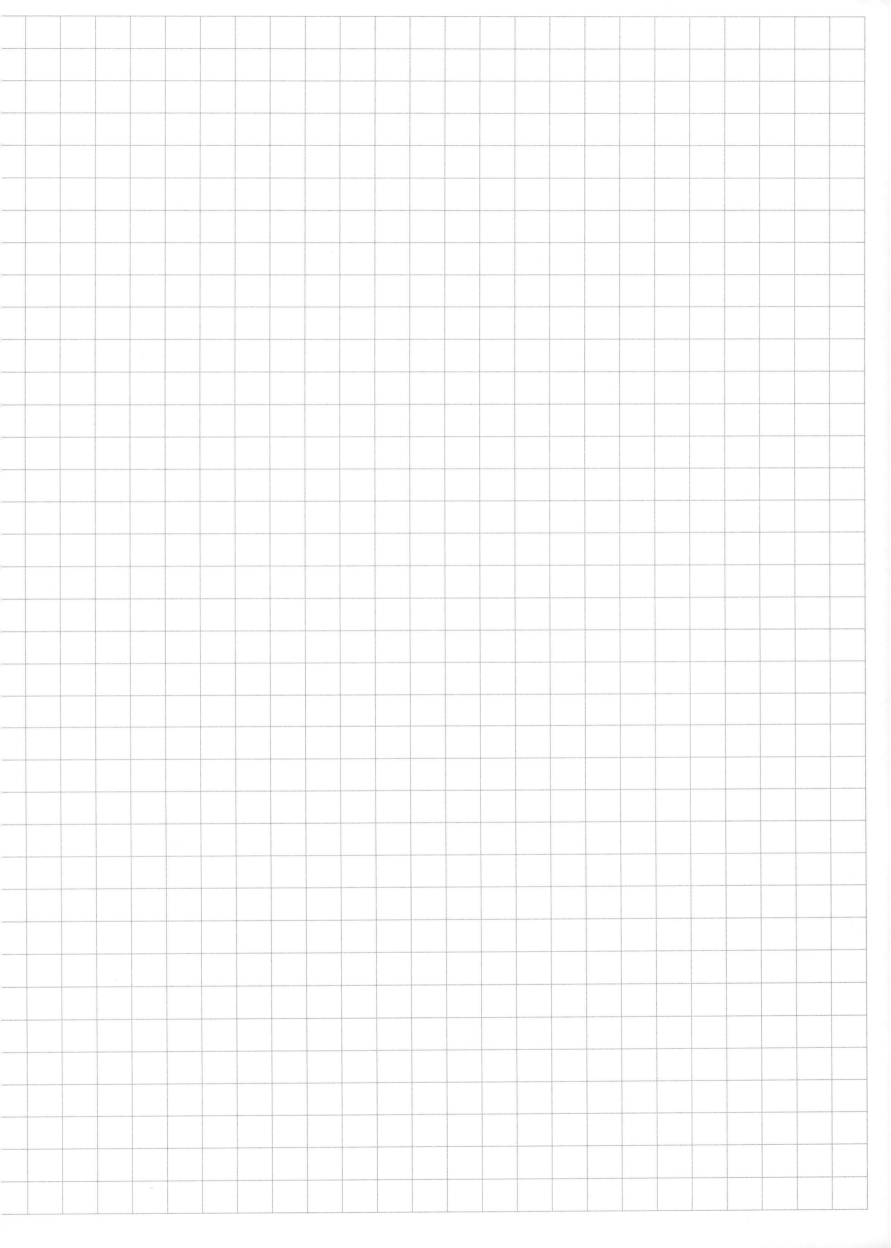

25

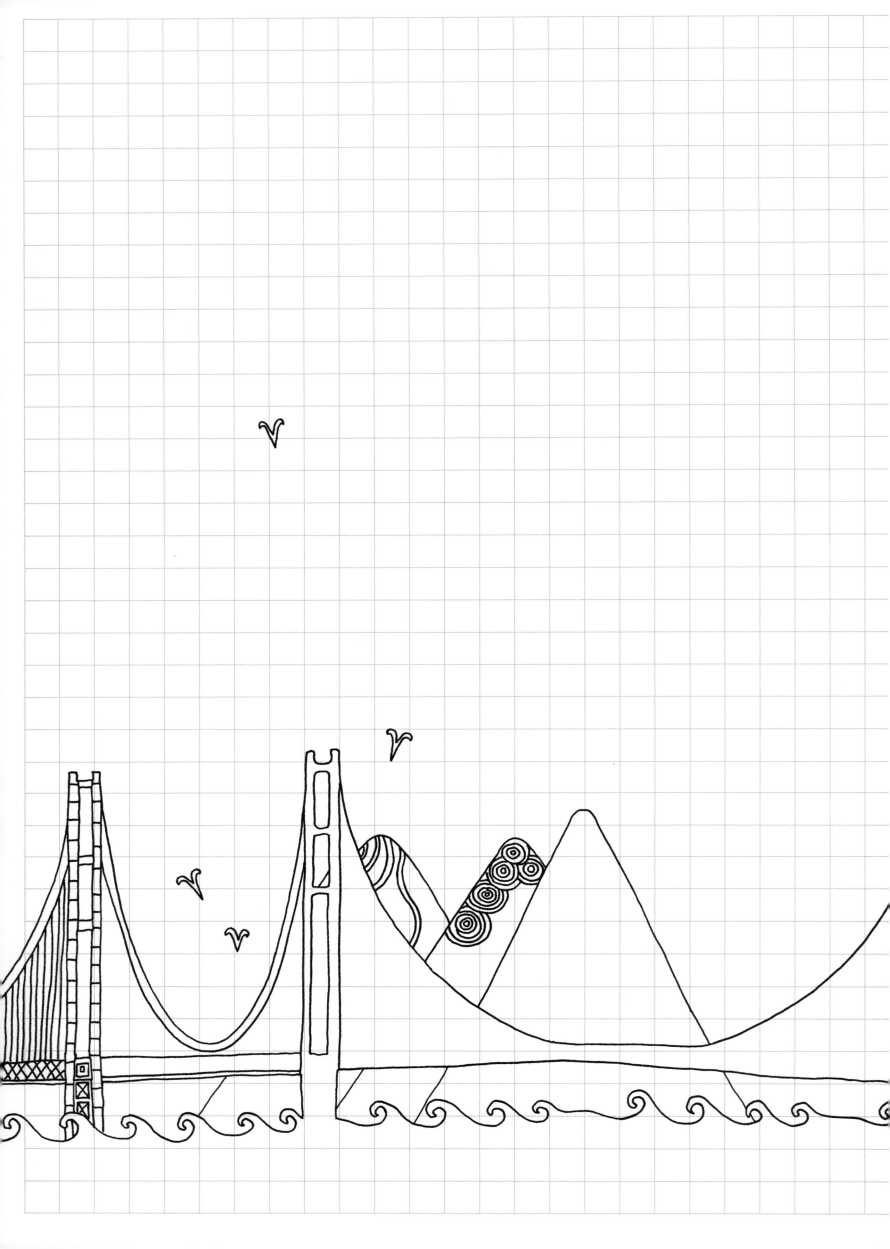

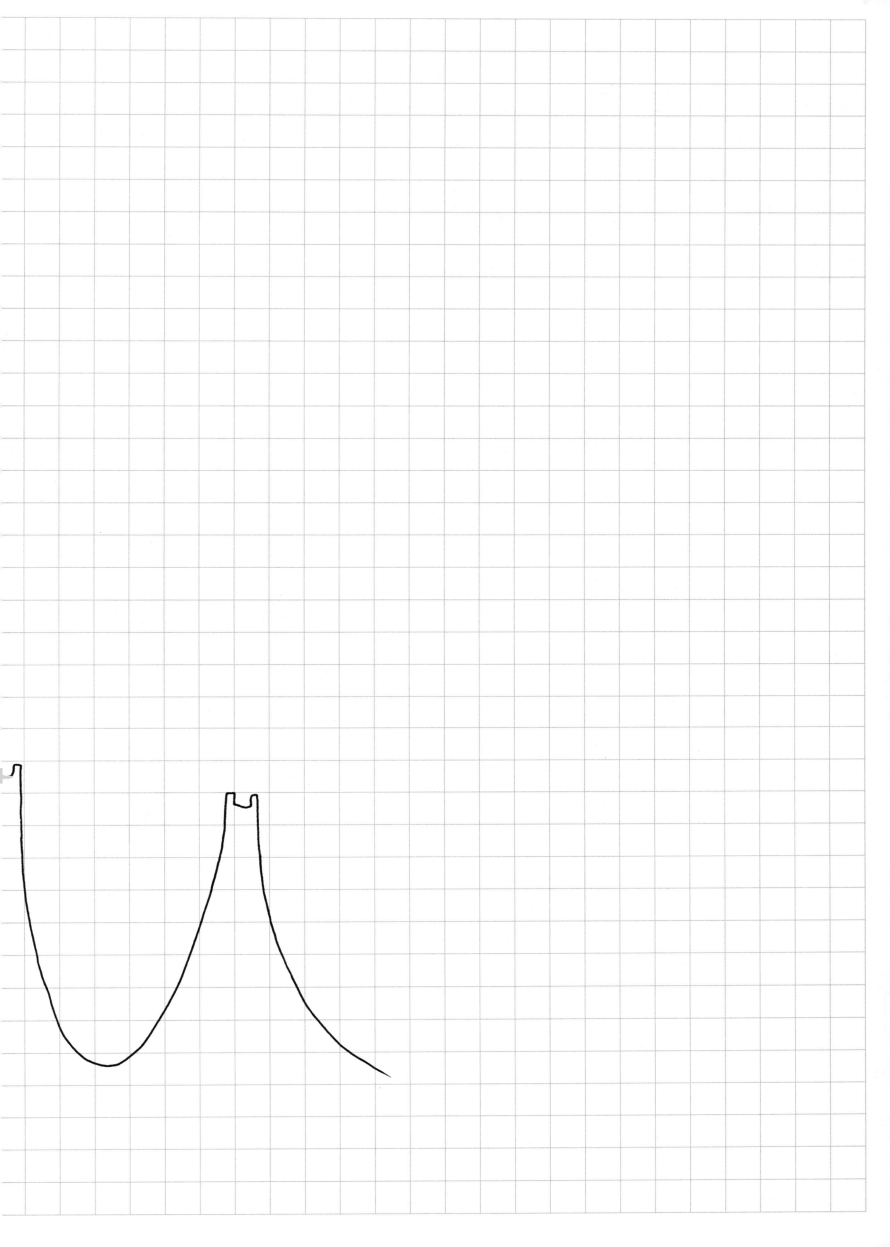

HOLLYWOOD

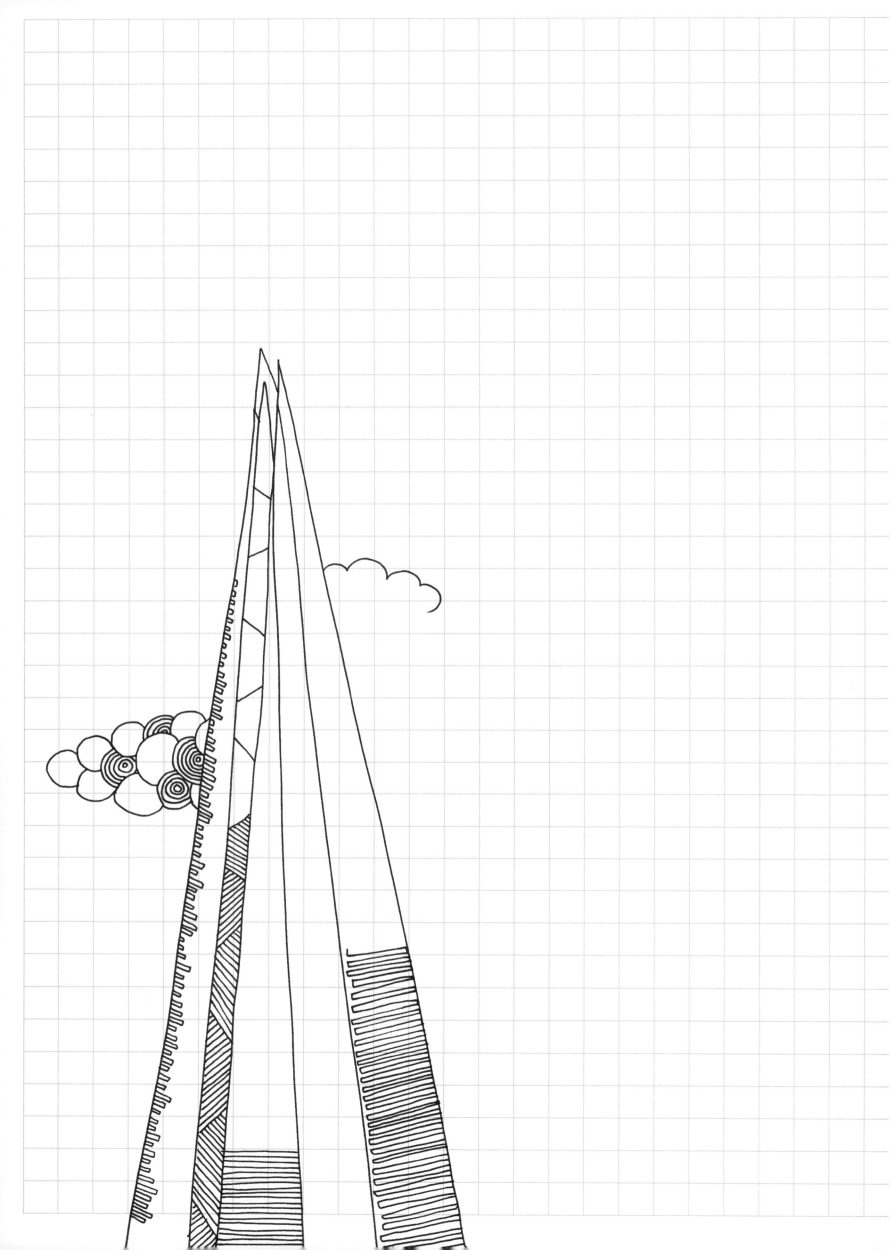

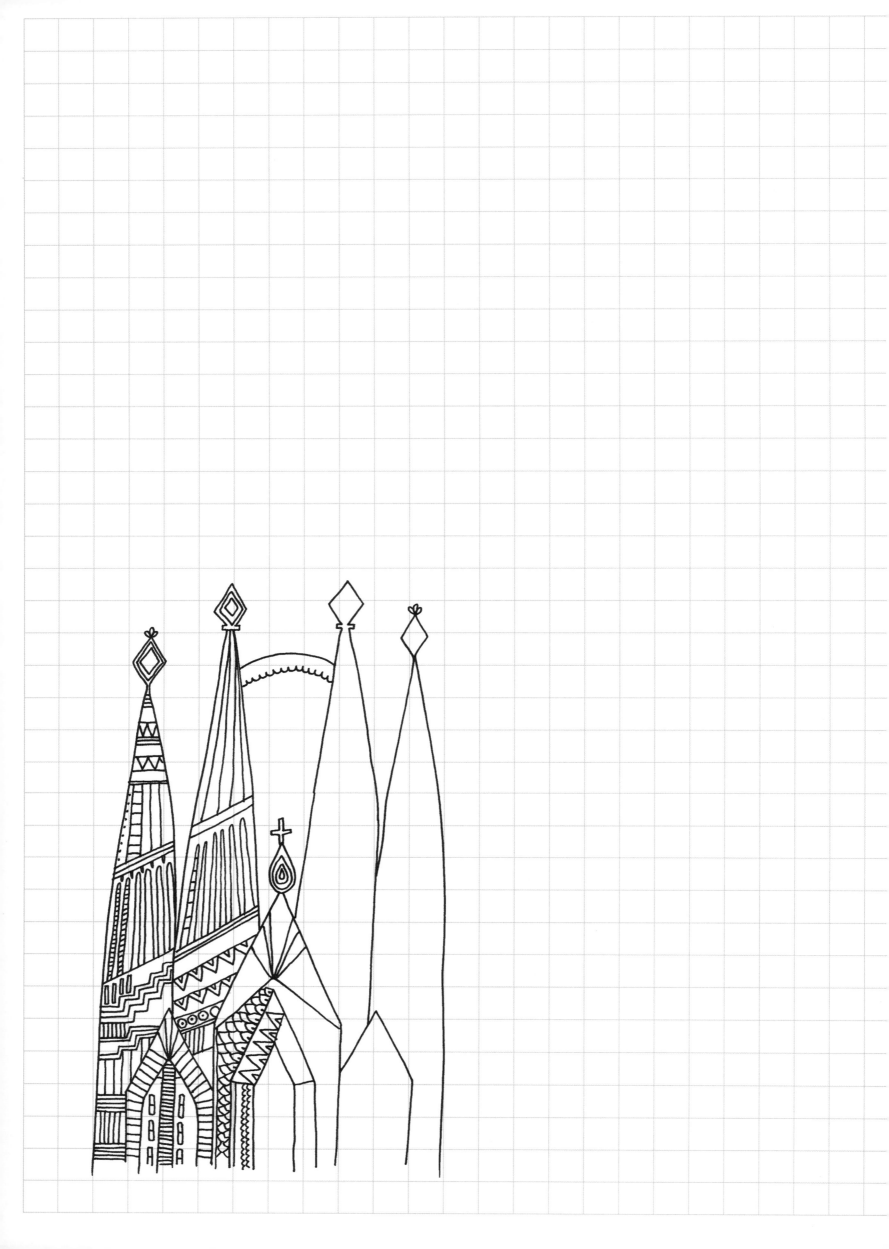

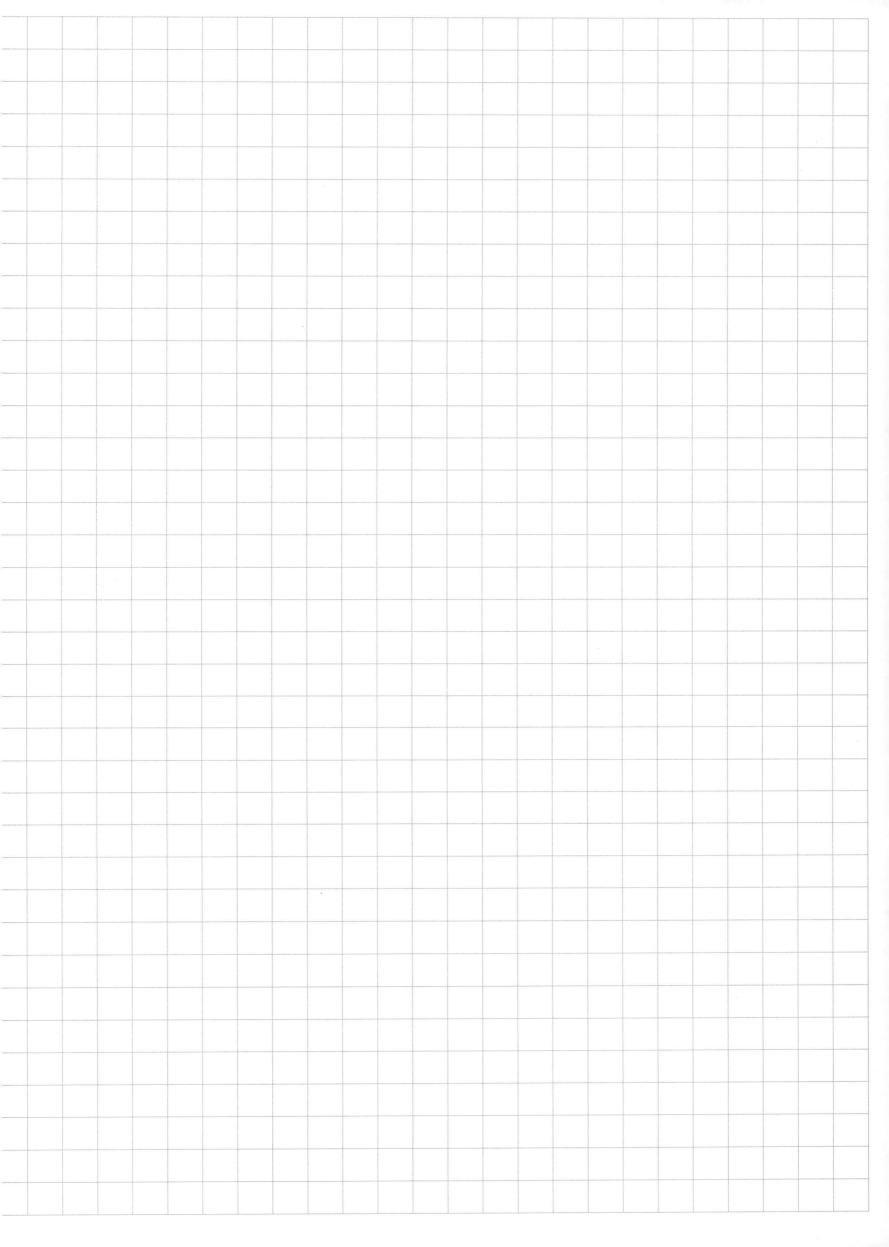

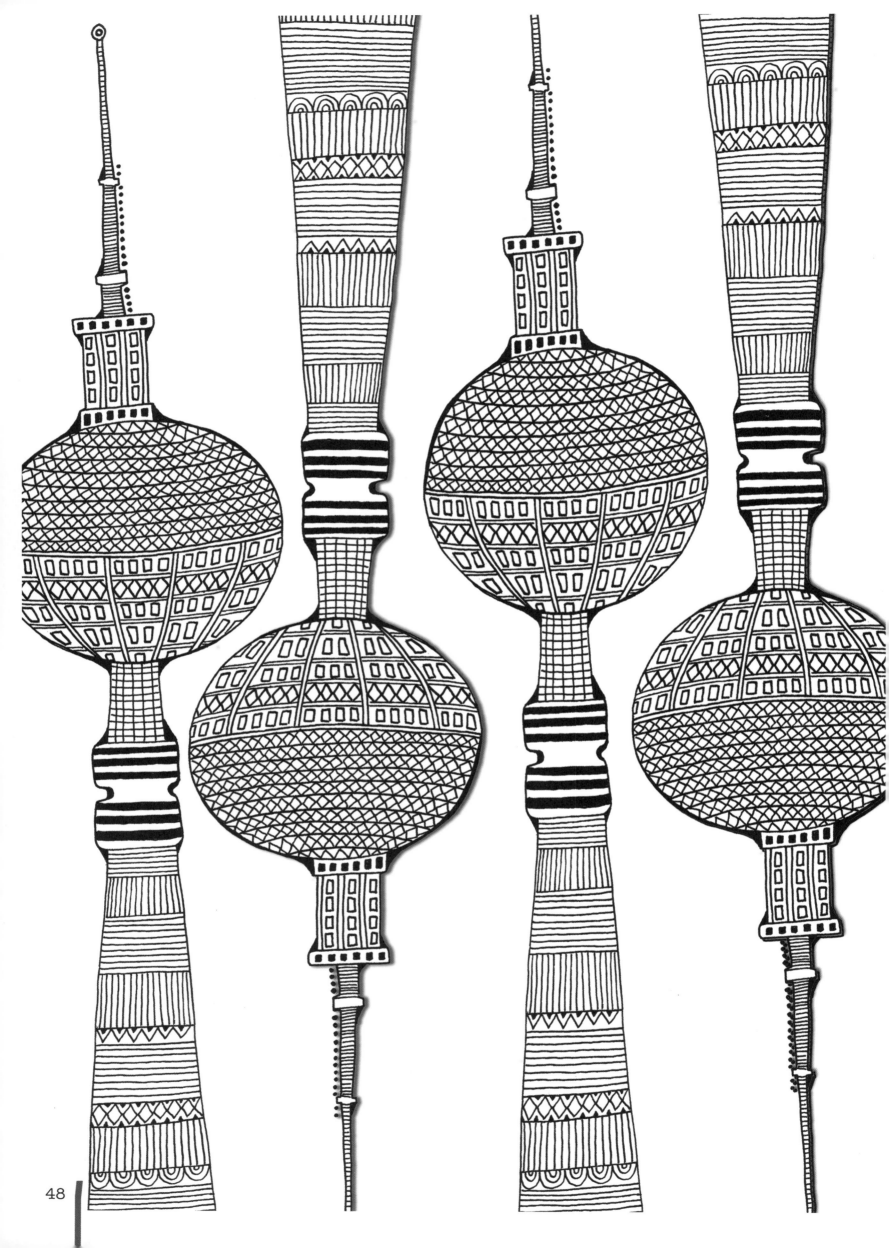

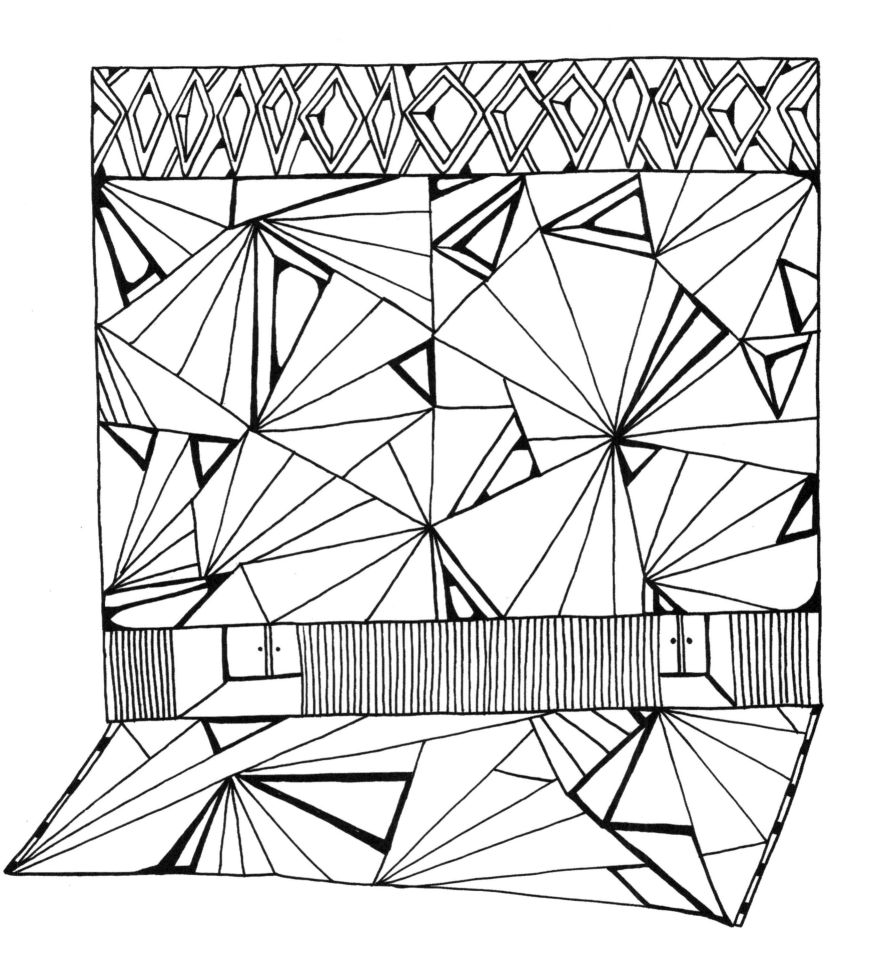

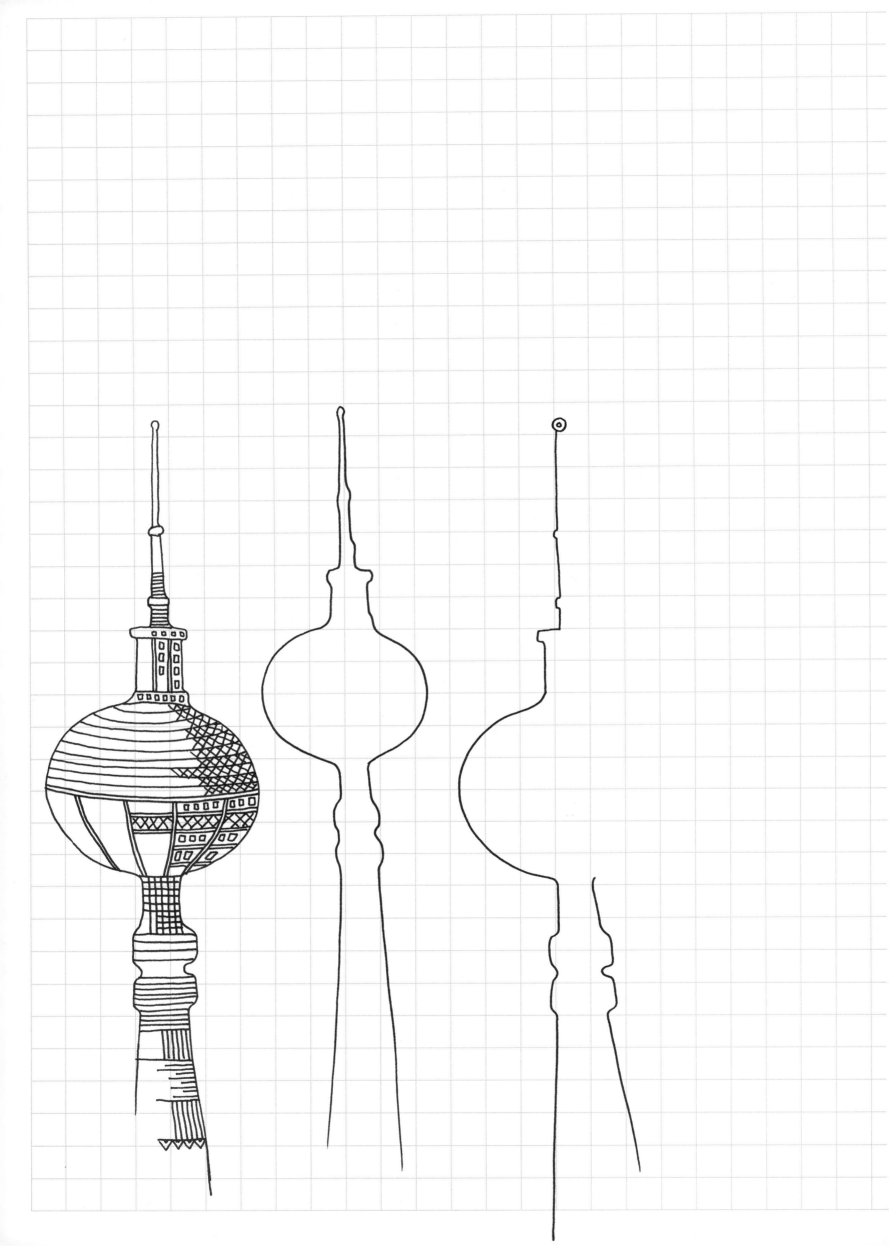

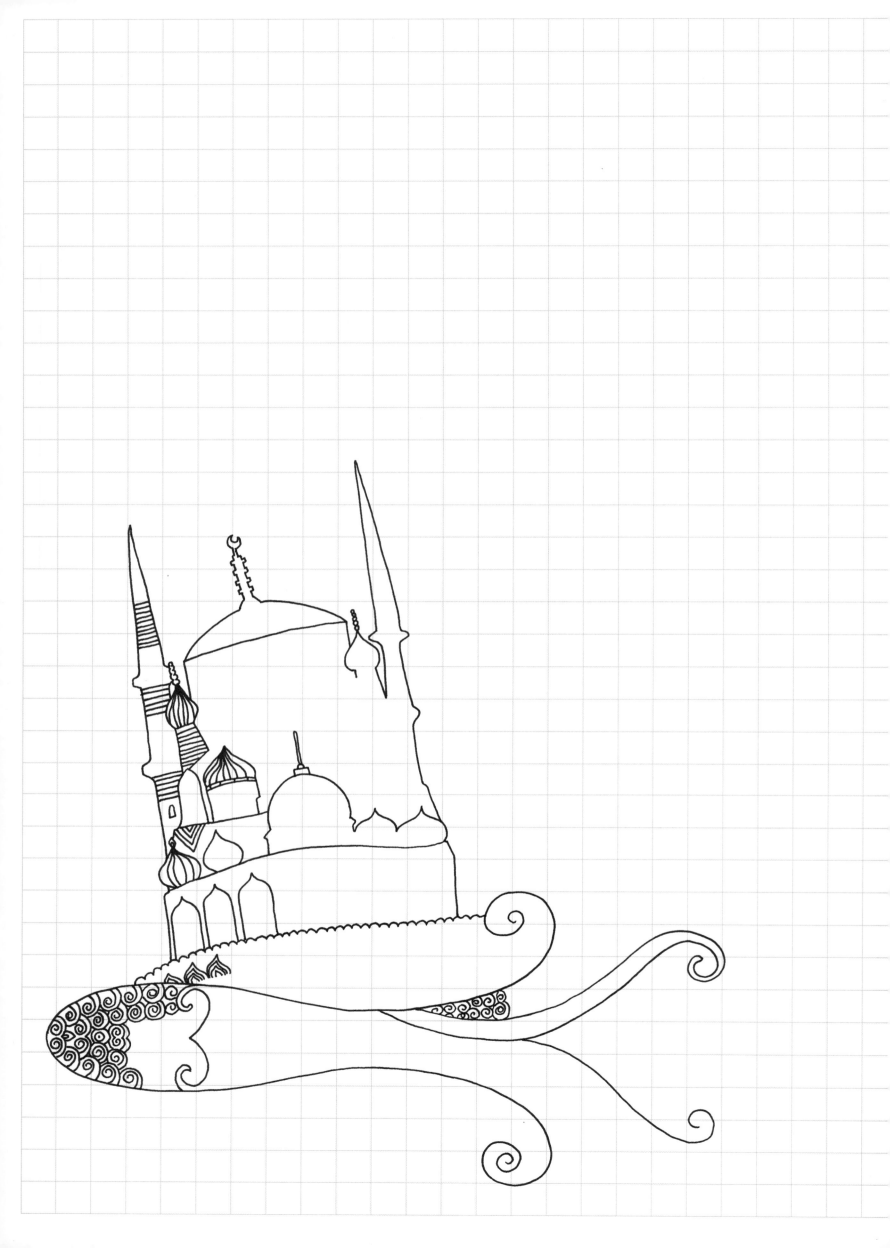

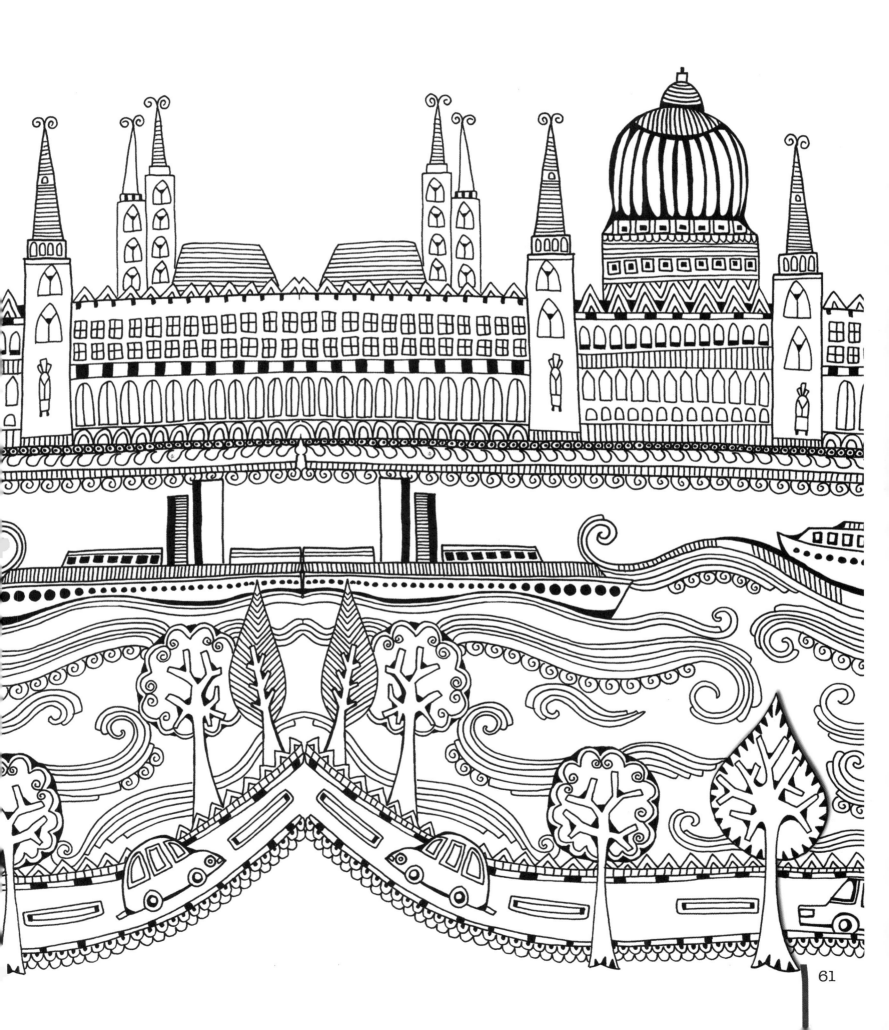

64

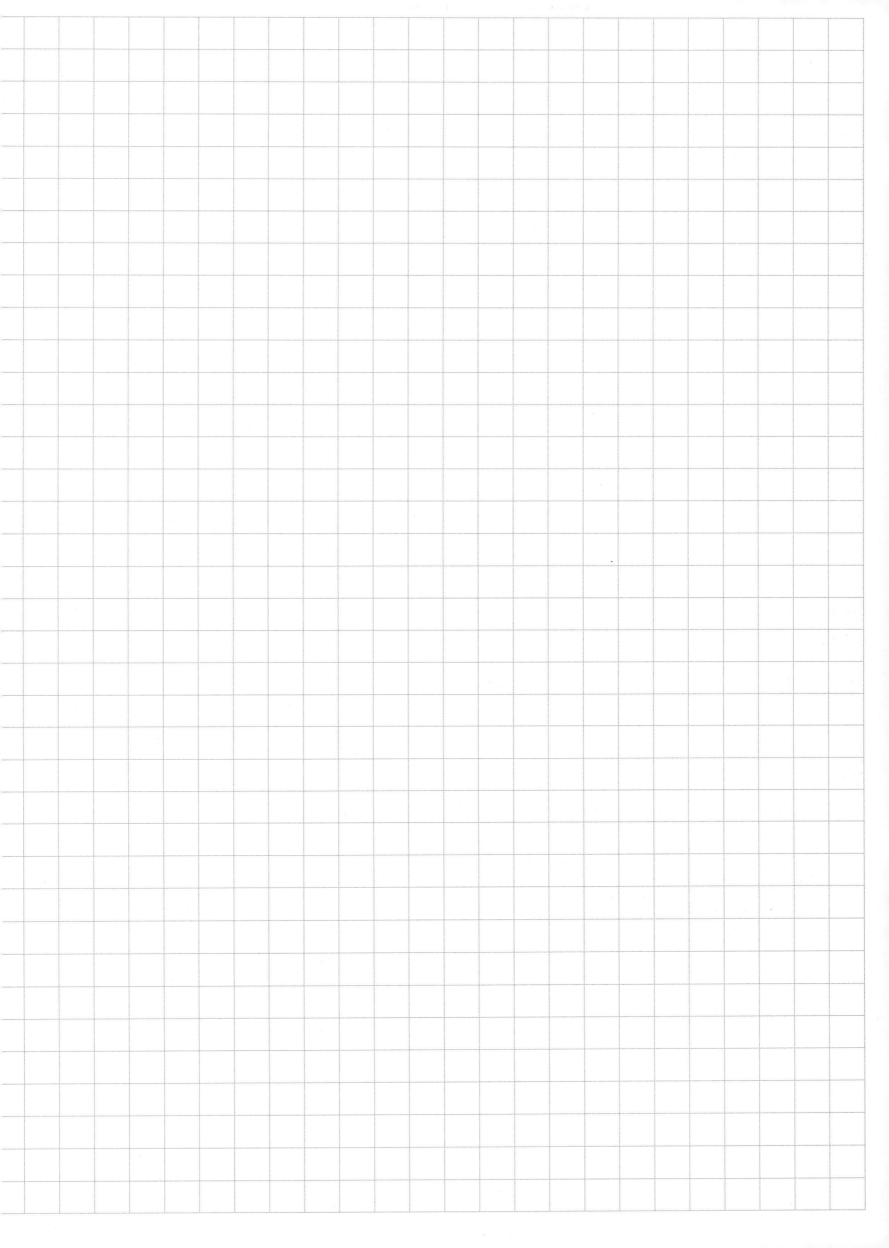

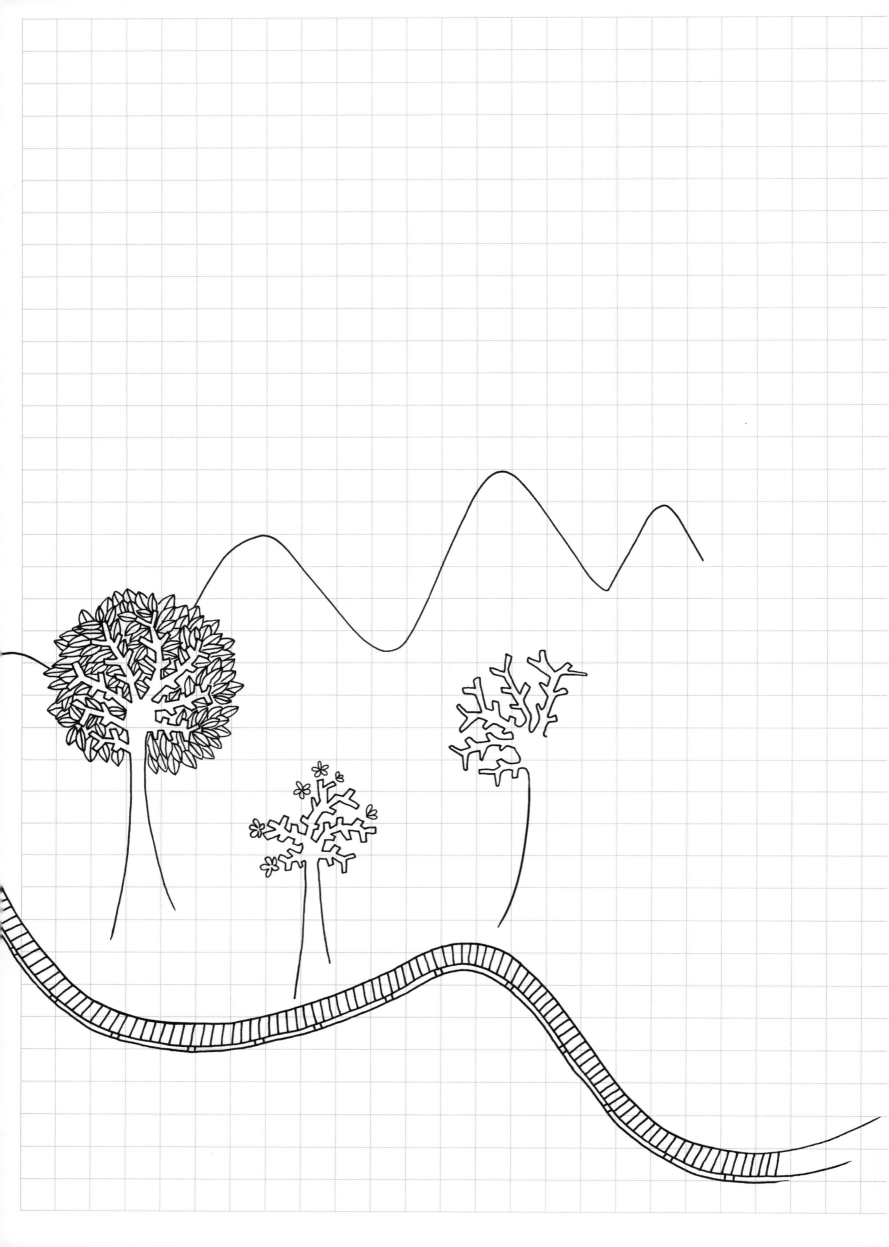

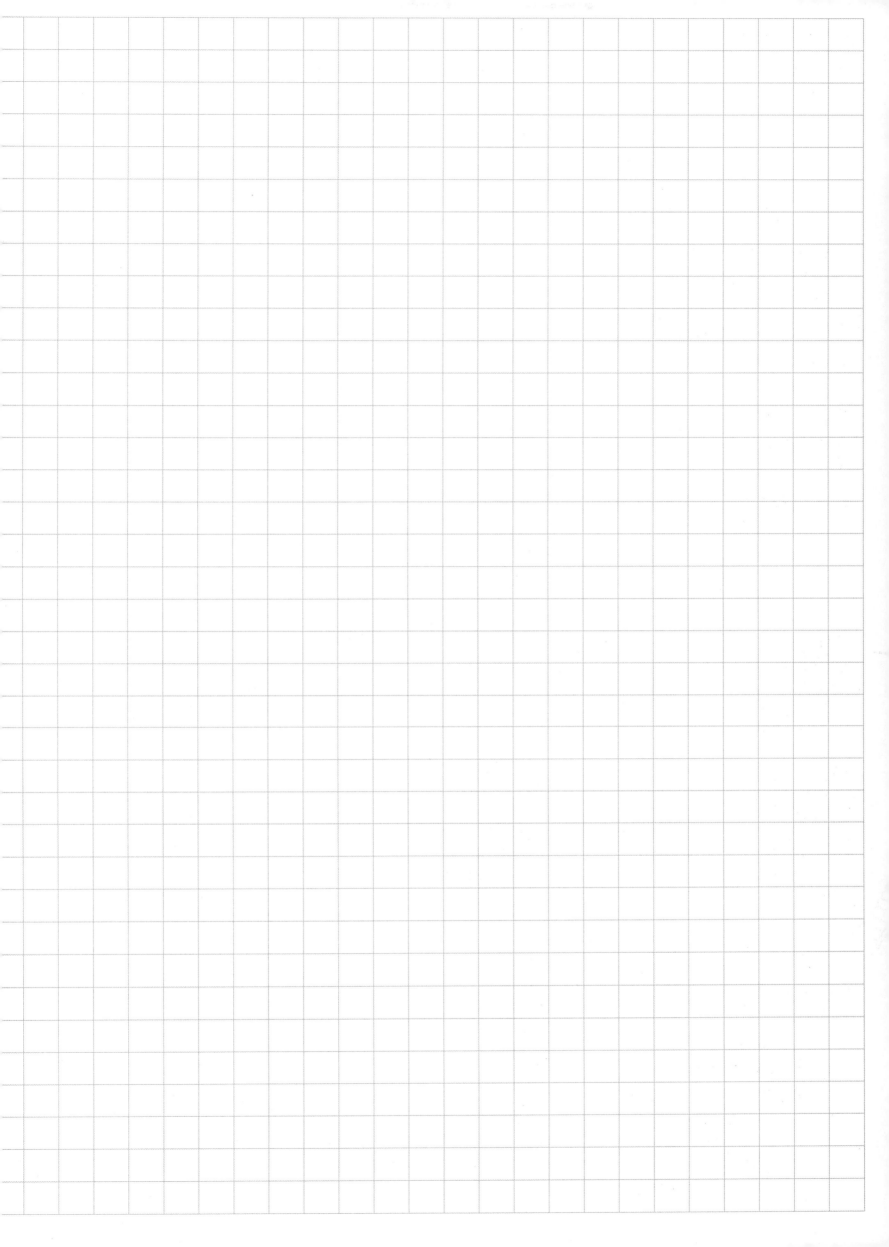

77

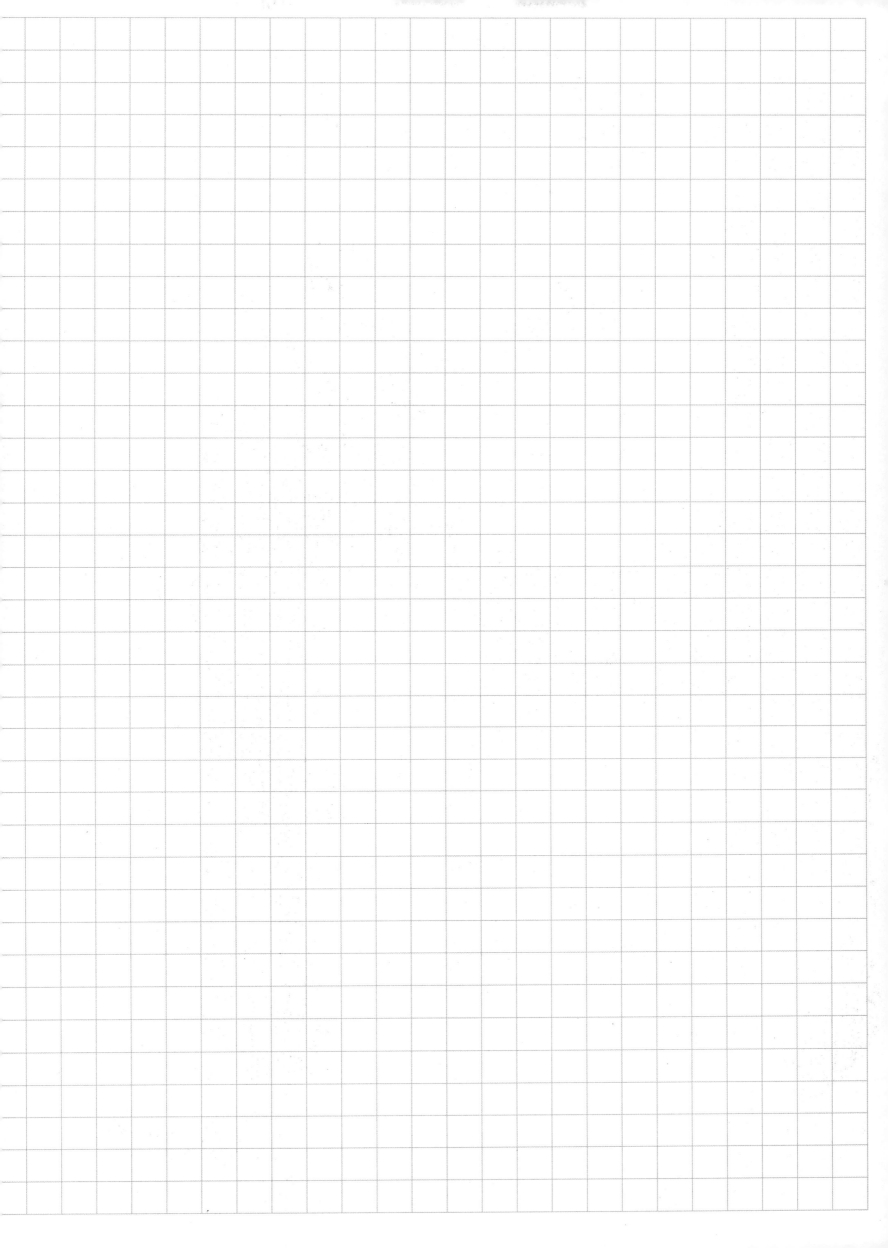

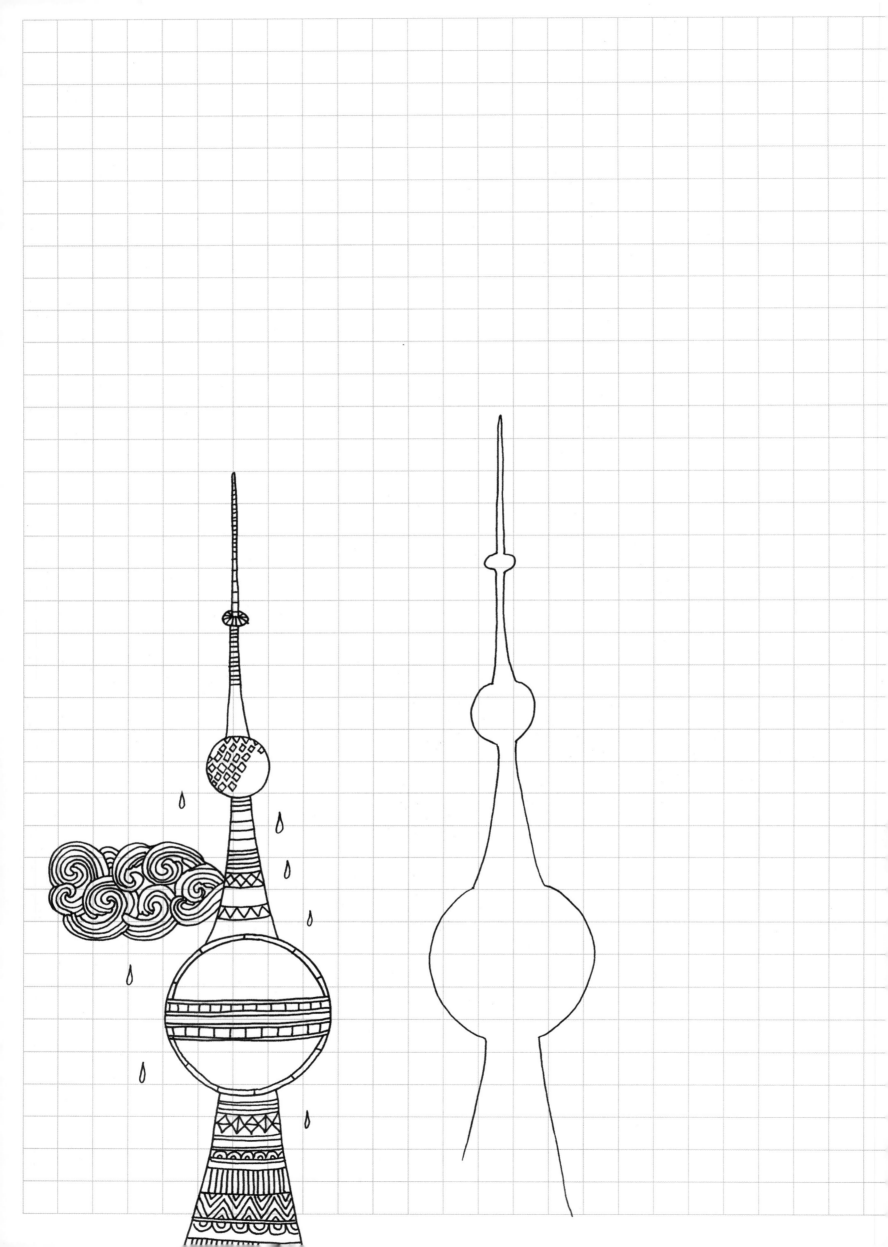

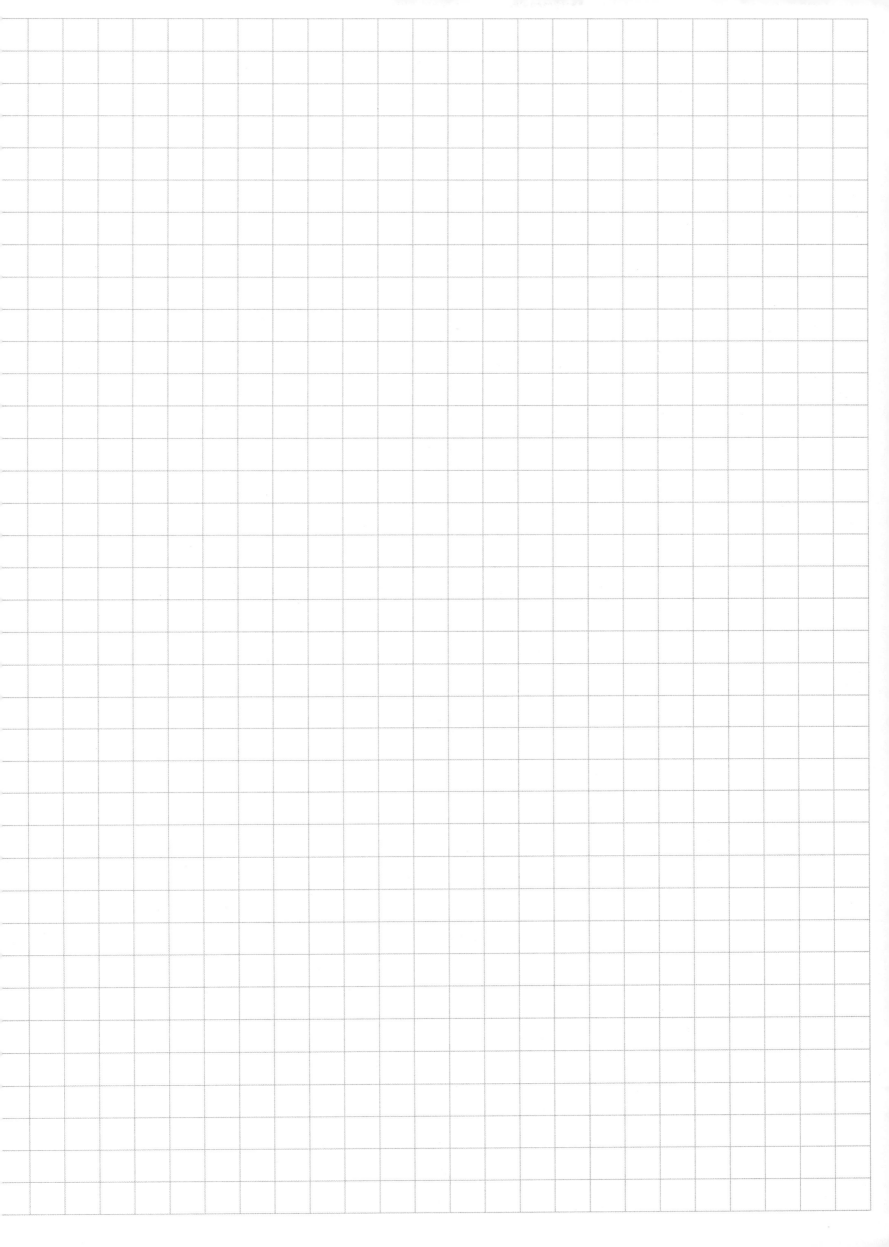

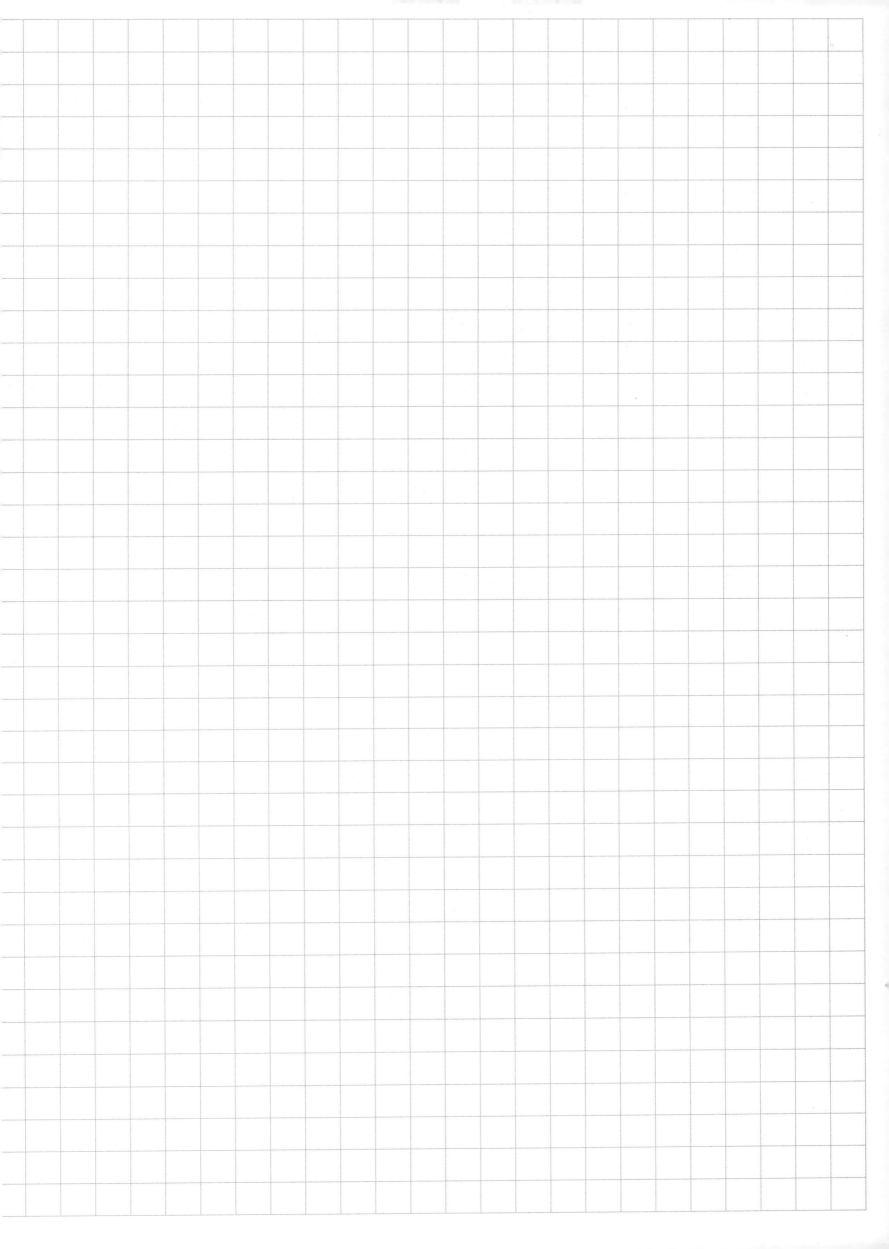

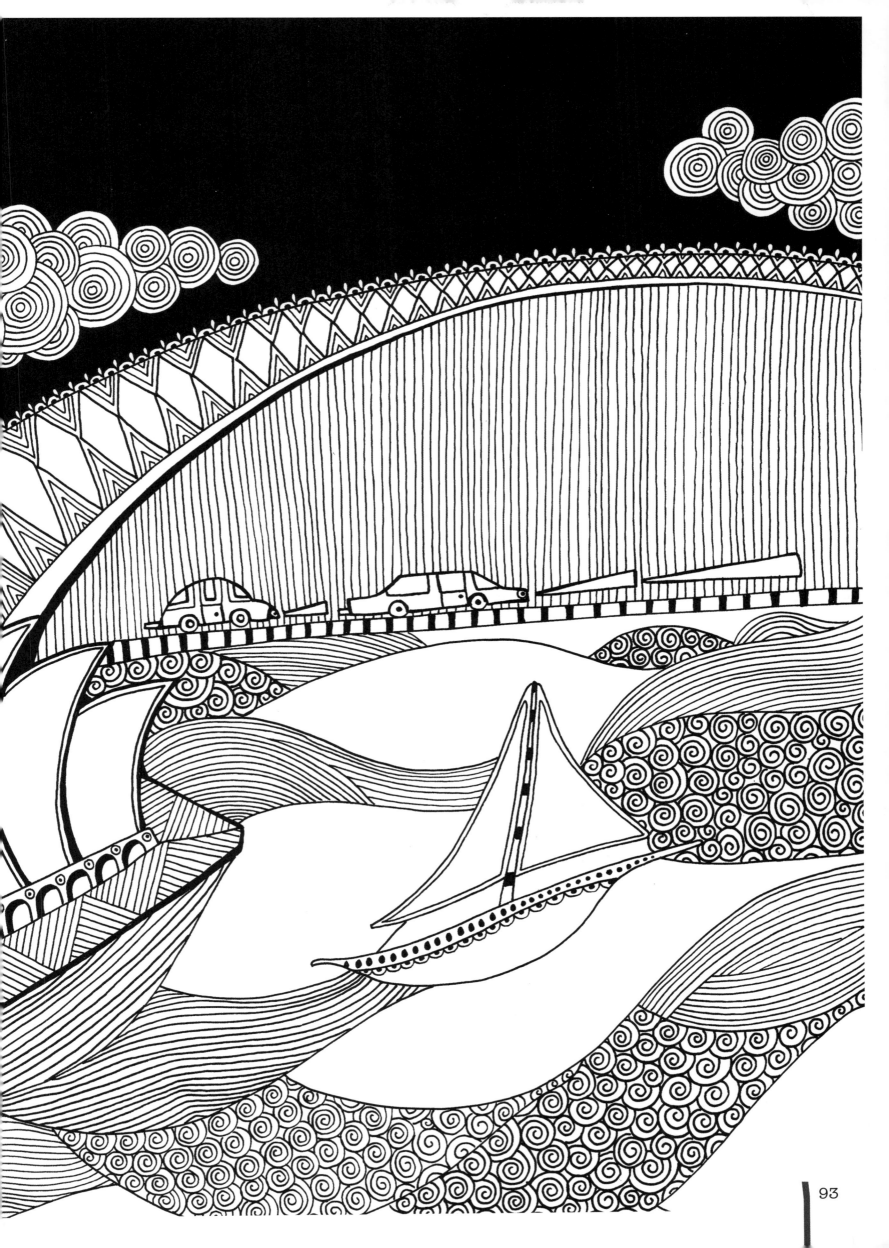

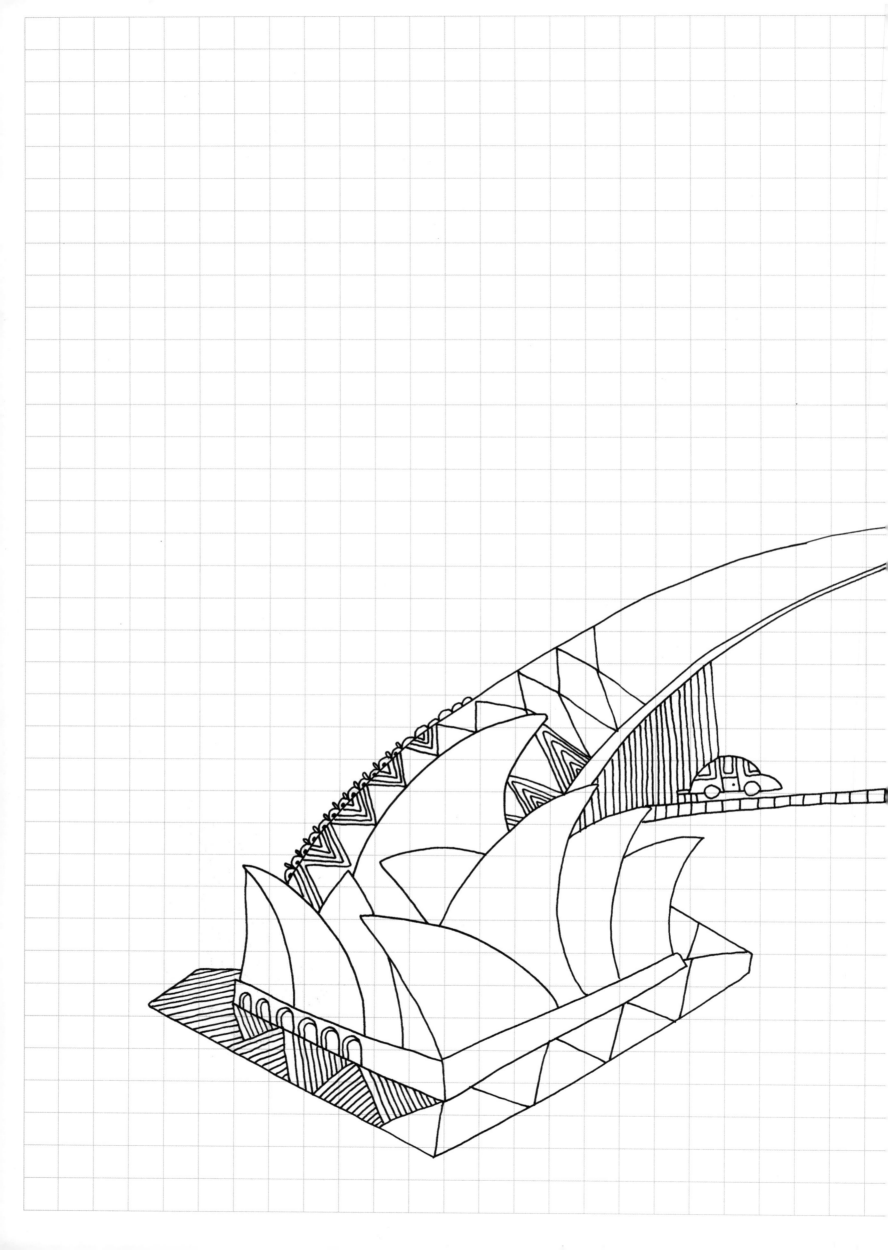

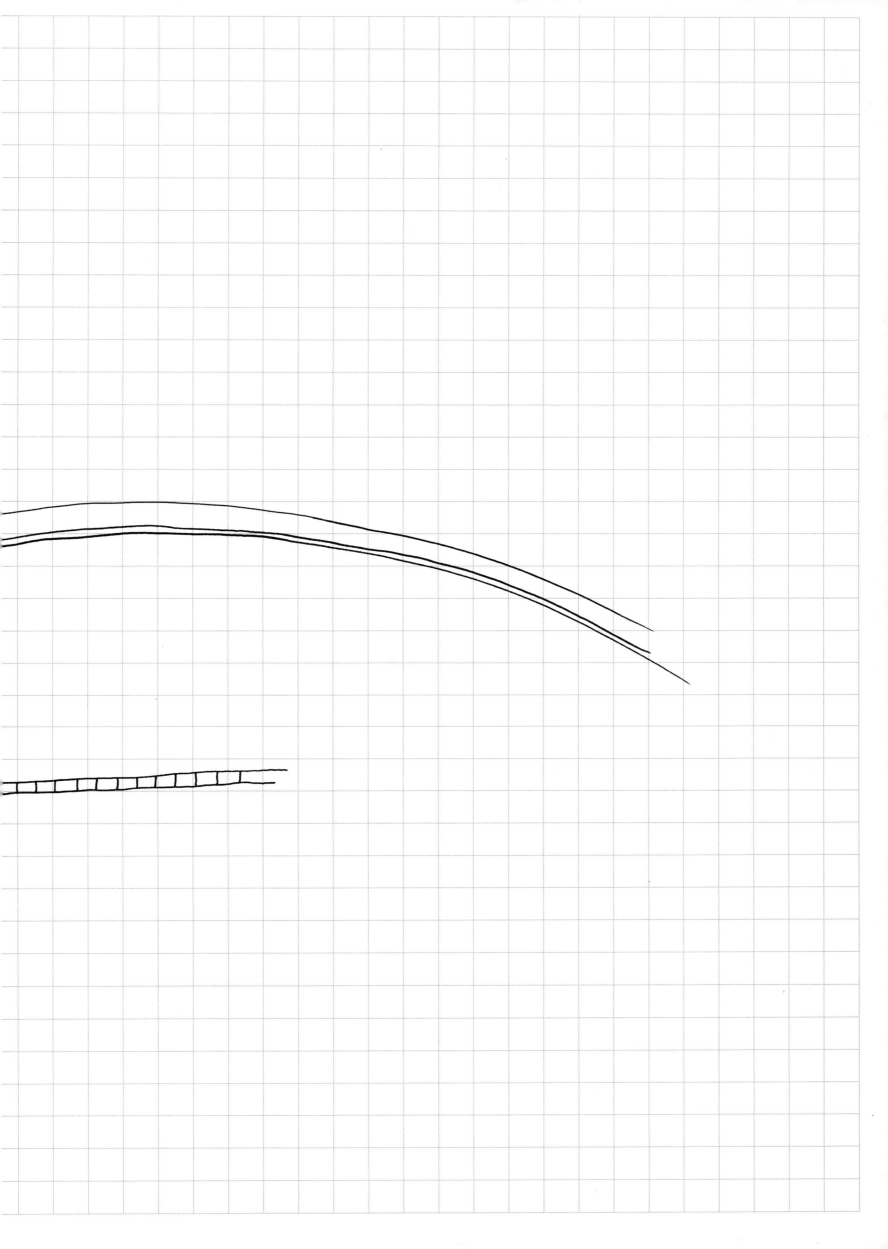